Claude

The Magician of Colour

Stephan Koja
Katja Miksovsky

Prestel
Munich · London · New York

A Childhood at the Seaside

Claude Monet was born in Paris on 14 November 1840. When he was five years old, his family moved to Le Havre on the north coast of France. He grew up in this lovely seaside town with its constantly changing light and the flowing patterns made by the water.

The fishermen were his friends. The young Monet spent many hours on the beach watching them work in the harbour.

Hauling a Boat Ashore, Honfleur

Later, when he had grown up, Monet painted this picture of three fishermen hauling their boat in at dawn. The sun has not risen yet, but its golden glow has already made the sky yellow and the bands of cloud are violet and red. A lighthouse looms in the background. The morning light is reflected in the water.

A caricature of a
man in a straw hat

A postcard showing
Honfleur near Le Havre

At about the time he started school, Monet began to draw the ships in the harbour and the many different types of people that arrived on them.

He was especially pleased when one of his caricatures of a fellow student or citizen of Le Havre earned him some pocket money. The owner of an artists' supply shop permitted Monet to display these caricatures in his window. They were shown in gold frames and new pictures were substituted every Sunday. Monet said later that he was filled with pride when he saw how people pressed their noses to the window to see his latest displays and to argue about how good the likenesses were.

The famous landscape painter Eugène Boudin also saw and liked these drawings. He invited Monet to join him on the beach to paint. But Monet did not want to do this. It was unusual for an artist to paint pictures in the open air, and the people of Le Havre thought that Boudin was a bit of a fool. One day, however, Monet went along with him. What he learned that day was to remain with him through his entire life. Painting fascinated him so much that he decided to become a painter. His parents were not convinced. They wanted him to enter a respectable profession and earn a decent living.

Monet Becomes a Painter

Monet made up his mind. In 1860, at the age of twenty, he travelled to Paris and began to study at one of the inexpensive art schools. His father was pretty annoyed. Only Monet's aunt, Marie-Jeanne Lecadre, who had looked after him since the death of his mother three years earlier, encouraged him and gave him a bit of money. When after a year in Paris he was called up to do his military service, she paid for an exemption so that he could complete his studies. Presumably, she understood his love of painting so well because she herself liked to paint. Above all, she believed that he had talent and that he would, one day, be a famous painter — and in that she was absolutely right!

Monet's fellow students at art school reported that he always wore elegant clothes. Even when he had no money — and this was almost always the case — he would appear in a lace-trimmed shirt, wearing a hat and carrying a walking stick.

Monet when he was about twenty-four

The Frog Pond *(La Grenouillère)*

Together with some of his painter-friends, Monet often travelled around the countryside near Paris, to the forests of Barbizon and Fontainebleau, where he painted large pictures in the open air. He painted the landscape and the Parisians who — as they still do today – went to the country to escape from the hectic life of the city.

This place painted by Monet was called the Frog Pond where there was a popular café on its banks. As you can see, Parisians did not wear hiking clothes on their outings, but promenaded through the countryside in their fashionable city clothes. It was considered the height of fashion to always carry small pastel parasols and to wear sun hats.

Springtime

On his trips to the countryside, Monet was often accompanied by his friend Camille Doncieux, later to become his wife, who would sit reading under a tree while he painted.

The Lunch:
Six-year-old Jean at lunch in the garden

The Family

In 1867, Camille gave birth to a son, Jean. At this time, Monet was selling very few pictures and was concerned about whether he could support his family. He regularly had to borrow money from friends and acquaintances. His friend Auguste Renoir, who was also a painter and who lived nearby, provided the young family with food. When Monet received a major commission from his dealer, he was able to enjoy a carefree few months with his family. He captured these happy times in several paintings.

The Evening Meal:
Jean, Camille (with her back to us), and two guests at the table, lit by a gas lamp

Monet as an Impressionist

What is an Impressionist?

The Impressionists typically liked to paint outdoors, and their pictures show everyday things. They particularly wanted to capture the beauty of lighting effects and the play of colour. Often, this was only a matter of a beautiful instant, and that is why many of their pictures were painted very quickly. Today, this seems entirely normal. In earlier times, however, pictures were painted in studios, where models in costumes stood motionless for hours in front of backdrops, so that paintings could be made depicting major events from mythology or history. Compared with these, of course, the Impressionists' pictures seemed pretty unusual!

Originally the word "Impressionist" was a nickname. In 1874, a critic had used it to describe the young artists who were exhibiting their modern pictures in Paris for the first time. The picture that inspired the nickname was *Monet's Impression — Soleil levant*, which means "Impression — Sunrise". It is reproduced on the left.

This picture was painted at Christmas, when Monet was in Le Havre for a few days. When he looked out of his window, he could see the harbour filled with ships and cranes. He got up early and painted the sunrise. The red sun rose into the grey-blue morning and shone on the little waves — painted with many small brush strokes. Three boats sail away from the bigger ships; they appear black against the dawning light. It seems that Monet completed the picture very quickly, since it was painted with few brush strokes and thick pigments. He wanted to capture the few minutes of sunrise with the morning light and fog over the water.

As a companion piece, he painted the harbour again, at night.

Impression — Sunrise

The Port of Le Havre, Night Effect

The Gare Saint-Lazare, the Normandy Train

Many people felt that the Impressionists' pictures were perplexing and thought they were only looking at quick sketches. They also thought that what they saw in the pictures was not pretty enough. Filthy steam trains! The public wanted to see majestic kings, lovely princesses, heroic wars, or scenes from the Bible, not everyday things!

Why, then, did Monet paint everyday things? Because he wanted to be a modern artist who painted the world he lived in. For that reason, he created paintings of the railway, one of the most recent triumphs of technology. He loved trains. He painted them again and again, sometimes crossing bridges, other times with smoking locomotives or arriving at the stations of Paris. While he was working on a series of pictures of the Saint-Lazare Station, the directors of the railroad even stopped trains for him, emptied the platforms of travellers, and heated up the boilers of the locomotives to create as much steam as possible.

Edouard Manet: *Monet Painting in his Studio Boat*

The Impressionists especially loved to visit the forests near Paris to paint. The painting below shows Monet with his easel at the forest's edge. But most of all, he loved to be near water. In 1872, he bought a boat and added a roof to make it into a studio. He would drift down the river in it or row along until he found something he wanted to paint. His artist friend Edouard Manet once painted him on his studio boat.

It was not especially comfortable to paint pictures outdoors. An artist had to carry all of his equipment with him: an easel on which to put canvases, a stool to sit on, a palette on which to mix colours, brushes and tubes of paint and, often, a sunshade.

John Singer Sargent:
Claude Monet,
Painting at the Edge of the Forest

Every year, there was a large art exhibition at the Salon in Paris. For many years, this had been the only place where the public could see new paintings. The judges at the Salon decided which pictures would be exhibited and which would not. The Impressionists' pictures were always rejected, because members of the Salon jury had old-fashioned ideas about art. Since the Impressionists did not exhibit at the Salon, they did not become known very quickly and had difficulty selling their pictures.

The Salon jury

Camille on her Death Bed, 1879

Difficult Times

In late summer 1878, Monet and his wife Camille — they had married against the wishes of Monet's father — travelled to Vétheuil together with their sons Jean and Michel. In this small community on the River Seine, they rented a house together with their friends Ernest and Alice Hoschedé and their six children.

It was a difficult time, since Camille was very sick, and her condition worsened daily. Monet tried desperately to sell his pictures to get money for the medicines she needed. Together with Alice, he spent long hours looking after his wife. He found no time for painting or earning a living.

After a long illness, Camille died. She was only thirty-two. Monet painted her on her death bed. He missed her so much that he almost lost his mind in the months that followed. The Hoschedés were also having a bad time. They had become very rich and then lost all of their money. So Ernest Hoschedé went to Paris to find a new job.

Peace and quiet finally returned after all the troubles, and Monet began to paint again. Alice looked after him and the children. Ernest Hoschedé never returned to Vétheuil and, following his death a few years later, Monet and Alice married.

Alice, around 1900

Vétheuil

The Road to Vétheuil

A dusty road ran in gentle curves to the town of Vétheuil, where Monet spent both good and bad times. For many years, he lived in a house at the side of the road where it entered the town. A garden running down to the Seine on the other side of the road belonged to the property, and Monet kept his boat tied up there.

Monet painted the town of Vétheuil on numerous occasions. In the picture above, we find ourselves in the middle of a beautiful autumn day, sometime toward dusk. How do we know this? The magic of this painting lies in the fact that we can sense the sun without seeing it.

The Road to Vétheuil, Snow Effect

Monet's house at the entrance to Vétheuil

Vétheuil Church

Monet Becomes Famous

Monet at forty

Monet became famous and many people visited him in his studio in Giverny, including the Duke of Trévise

After many years of bitter struggle during which Monet and all the other Impressionist painters received little public recognition and were unable to sell their pictures, things began to look up.

Monet was already forty years old when his art achieved recognition. Suddenly, everyone wanted to buy his pictures — not only in Paris, where his dealer had his shop, but also abroad, especially in America.

Bordighera
painted looking towards the Mediterranean

The Aiguille (Needle) and the Falaise d'Aval at Etretat:
Monet's painting (above) and a photograph (below)

Monet was more famous for the pictures he did on trips to the seaside than for any others.

When painting, he was prepared for every eventuality. On the Atlantic coast, he was bothered by the wind and freezing temperatures. He fastened his easel to the ground with ropes and pegs so it would not fall over.

Often, he clambered down to the beach over steep cliffs carrying all of his equipment. Once when he was painting at the water's edge, he became so involved in his work that he did not see an enormous wave, which hurled him against the cliffs and carried all his things out to sea. Monet came close to drowning. When he climbed out of the water, his beard and jacket were covered with paint from his palette; the picture he had been working on and his easel had been crushed by the roaring waves.

Monet's house in Giverny with the wheatstacks

In 1883, Monet, Alice, and their children moved to Giverny, a small town near Paris. One evening, Monet went out to the field behind the house to paint the wheatstacks that the farmers had made after the harvest to store grain for the winter. He began to paint, but quickly realised that the colours he saw were being transformed by the sun, so that suddenly his picture did not look like what he was seeing in the field. He sent one of his daughters home to fetch another canvas for a new picture. Instead of the wheat-stacks, he wanted to paint the sun and the light that surrounded him and changed their colours.

Monet made many famous pictures of wheatstacks at many different times of year and times of day. On the left is a wheatstack at sunset. It seems almost to be burning — the setting sun has transformed the colours and made everything yellow and red. The picture below was painted in winter, and the ground is covered with snow.

Wheatstacks on a summer evening (left) and in winter (below)

Why did Monet always paint the same subject, only with different colours?

Rouen Cathedral

Monet's cathedral paintings also became world-famous. He painted the church in the French city of Rouen from a clothing shop opposite it. When he began to paint in the morning, the cathedral appeared blue in the early light. But soon the light — and the colours — changed. The stone wall became a pale yellow, and Monet started a new canvas in order to record this view. The warmth of the afternoon sun and the red light of dusk bathed the cathedral in rosy tones. So Monet made more paintings — eighteen in all. He could only work on each painting for a very short time, and so he completed this series of pictures in a single week. Details are much easier to make out in the photograph above than in the paintings. But, as if by magic, Monet captured the colours of an entire day in his paintings.

Rouen Cathedral on a grey morning, before noon, at noon, and (right) in the late afternoon

Happy Times in Giverny

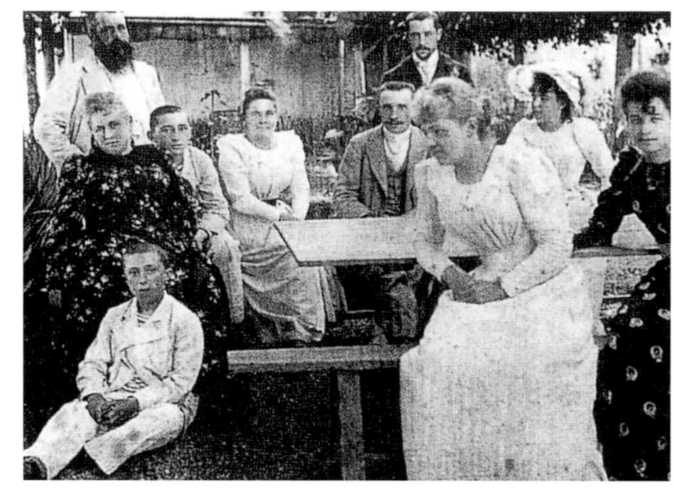

The family at Giverny: Monet stands at the rear left, in front of him Alice Hoschedé, at her feet Michel, next to her Jean-Pierre. The others, from left to right: Blanche, Jean, Jacques (standing), Marthe, Germaine, and Suzanne

Jean-Pierre and Michel, the youngest

Ice-skating on the Epte

It was a happy time in Giverny. The house was situated on a branch of the Seine and near another small river, the Epte. This was paradise for the children. They could bathe, sail, fish, and ice skate or help the farmers with the harvest.

Monet's greatest love was for flowers. Roses climbed the walls of his house, and he planted a thousand different types of flowers in his garden at Giverny. He loved flowers because their blooms were filled with bright colours. When he walked in his garden, he plunged into a multicoloured, perfumed sea of flowers.

The house at Giverny

Boat on the Epte

This painting of two girls in a boat is an especially lovely holiday picture. The girls are Marthe and Blanche Hoschedé, Alice's elder daughters. The girls' bright clothing is reflected in the water; light plays on their hats and dresses. It is summer. The boat glides silently past the shadowy foliage of bushes. The dark water seems mysterious, still, secretive. Time stands still.

The picture on the cover of this book shows Germaine, the youngest child, in a boat, and, sitting near her, Suzanne and Blanche.

Travels

Claude and Alice in the Piazza San Marco in Venice

The Houses of Parliament, London, Sun through Fog

Throughout his life, Monet made many trips to collect impressions for his pictures. He travelled along the Atlantic coast and to the Mediterranean, to Norway, Spain, London, and Venice. Alice often accompanied him, while one of the older children looked after the others. In Venice, where he painted the picture on the opposite page, he was photographed feeding pigeons.

Monet especially liked to paint London in the fog, which blanketed the city in misty light.

Palazzo Contarini del Zaffo in Venice

Charing Cross Bridge, the Thames

Monet in the car he bought in 1900 and which he drove over the Alps to Saint Moritz — in winter!

The lily pond at Giverny

The Water Lilies

At home in Giverny, Monet painted in the garden throughout the summer. He had waterproof equipment he left out in the garden during the warmest time of the year. Usually, he sat with his easel and a large umbrella on a high stool on the banks of his lily pond from where he could see the water's surface. Often, Alice or one of the children kept him company.

Monet, painting the lily pond, with Blanche

Water Lilies

Is this picture upside-down?
Which is the top and which is the bottom?

Since we know the picture's title,
we can figure out the puzzle.

The lily pond was the focus of Monet's garden. He had difficulties with the local farmers when he was laying it out. They were afraid that the plants in the pond might poison their animals who might drink from the stream that flowed through it. Their wives worried that the water would not be any good for washing laundry. The farmers thought the painter was strange in any case. He painted instead of working, and they could not understand his fascination with flowers. Finally, Monet received permission to create his pond, and none of the farmers' fears came true. When he looked out over the water, Monet saw clouds reflected among the willow branches, and he painted them again and again.

The Japanese Bridge

This is a Japanese bridge from a picture by the Japanese artist Hokusai

Monet not only bought exotic, rare, and often expensive water lilies from far away lands to plant in his lily pond; he also had a Japanese wooden bridge built over it. Japanese pictures often depicted bridges; Monet decorated his house with them, and they served as an inspiration for his own paintings. Monet particularly loved the view of his bridge and painted many pictures of it.

Monet near the Japanese bridge

This is how Monet painted the Japanese bridge a few years before his death

Farewell

Monet after an eye operation in February 1923

As Monet became older, his boat remained at its moorings more and more of the time. A doctor discovered that he had an illness that made people blind. Monet was very frightened of having an operation, because he feared that he would lose his sight entirely — an unbearable idea, especially for a painter!

In the end, he had three operations on his right eye and was extremely fortunate. He could see as well as before his illness.

View of Giverny

Monet died in 1926 at his house in Giverny at the age of eighty-six. Only days before, he had been delighted by the delivery of some Japanese lilies, his favourite flowers.

Many friends and acquaintances from near and far came to his funeral. Monet was already the most famous artist in the world.

Today, his house and garden at Giverny are a museum visited by people from all around the world.

Monet's funeral procession, 8 December 1926

The pictures in this book:

Cover:

In the Rowing-Boat (detail), 1887, oil on canvas, 38⅝ x 51⅝ in. (98 x 113 cm), Musée d'Orsay, Paris

A Childhood at the Seaside:

Hauling a Boat Ashore, Honfleur (detail), 1864, oil on canvas, 21¾ x 32⅜ in. (55.2 x 82.1 cm), Memorial Art Gallery of the University of Rochester, New York

Man with a Straw Hat (detail), *c.* 1875, pencil and gouache on paper, 9⅞ x 6⅜ in. (25 x 16 cm), Musée Marmottan, Paris

Honfleur, the coastline of St. Siméon, postcard, *c.* 1864

Seascape, Storm (detail), 1866/67, oil on canvas, 19⅛ x 25½ in. (48.7 x 64.7 cm), The Clark Art Institute, Williamstown, Massachusetts

Monet Becomes a Painter:

Monet, photograph by Etienne Carjat, *c.* 1864

La Grenouillère (detail), 1869, oil on canvas, 29⅜ x 39¼ in. (74.6 x 99.7 cm), The Metropolitan Museum of Art, New York

Springtime, 1872–74, oil on canvas, 19⅝ x 25⅝ in. (50 x 65 cm), The Walters Art Museum, Baltimore, Maryland

The Family:

The Lunch (detail), 1873, oil on canvas, 63¾ x 80 in. (162 x 203 cm), Musée d'Orsay, Paris

The Evening Meal, 1868/69, oil on canvas, 19⅞ x 25¾ in. (50.5 x 65.5 cm), Stiftung Sammlung E. G. Bührle, Zurich

Monet as an Impressionist:

Impression – Sunrise (detail), 1872, oil on canvas, 18⅞ x 24⅞ in. (48 x 63 cm), Musée Marmottan, Paris

The Port of Le Havre, Night Effect, 1873, oil on canvas, 23⅝ x 31⅞ in. (60 x 81 cm), Hasso Plattner Collection

The Gare Saint-Lazare, the Normandy Train (detail), oil on canvas, 23½ x 31⅝ in. (59.6 x 80.2 cm), The Art Institute of Chicago, Mr. and Mrs. Martin A. Ryerson Collection

Edouard Manet:
Monet Painting in his Studio Boat, 1874, oil on canvas, 32½ x 31⅝ in. (82.5 x 105. cm), Bayerische Staatsgemäldesammlungen, Neue Pinakothek, Munich; Photograpie Giraudon, Vanves, Bridgeman

John Singer Sargent
Claude Monet, Painting at the Edge of the Forest (detail), 1887, oil on canvas, 21¼ x 25½ in. (54 x 64.8 cm), Tate Gallery, London

The jury of the Salon, *c.* 1885

Difficult Times:

Camille on her Death Bed, 1879, oil on canvas, 35⅝ x 26¾ in. (90 x 68 cm), Musée d'Orsay, Paris

Alice Monet, photograph, *c.* 1900, Musée Marmottan, Académie des Beaux-Arts, Paris

Pears and Grapes (detail), 1880, oil on canvas, 31⅞ x 25⅝ in. (81 x 58 cm), Hamburger Kunsthalle, Hamburg

Vétheuil:

Vétheuil Church (detail), 1878, oil on canvas, 25⅝ x 21⅝ in. (65 x 55 cm), National Gallery of Scotland, Edinburgh
The Road to Vétheuil, 1880, oil on canvas, 23 x 28½ in. (58.4 x 72.3 cm), The Phillips Collection, Washington, D.C.

The Road to Vétheuil, Snow Effect, 1879, oil on canvas, 24 x 31⅛ in. (61 x 81.5 cm), Museum of Fine Arts, St. Petersburg, Florida, on loan from a private collection

Monet Becomes Famous:

Claude Monet, photograph, 1880

Visit of Duc de Trévise at Giverny, photograph, 1920

Bordighera, 1884, oil on canvas, 25⅝ x 31⅞ in. (65 x 81 cm), The Art Institute of Chicago, Mr. and Mrs. Potter Palmer Collection

The Aiguille and the Falaise d'Aval, 1885, oil on canvas, 25½ x 31⅞ in. (64.9 x 81.1 cm), The Clark Art Institute, Williamstown, Massachusetts

Etretat, the Needle (Aiguille) and the Falaise d'Aval, photograph

Pink and Blue Impression: Wheatstack (detail), 1890/91, oil on canvas, 28¾ x 36¼ in. (73 x 92 cm), private collection

Monet's house in Giverny with the wheatstacks, photograph, 1905

Wheatstack with Snow, Morning, 1890, oil on canvas, 25⅝ x 35¼ in. (65 x 92 cm), Museum of Fine Arts, Boston

Rouen Cathedral, photograph, *c.* 1890

Rouen Cathedral, 1894, oil on canvas, 39⅜ x 28¾ in. (100 x 73 cm), Musée des Beaux-Arts, Rouen

Rouen Cathedral, 1894, oil on canvas, 39⅜ x 28¾ in. (100 x 73 cm), The Norton Simon Foundation, Los Angeles

Rouen Cathedral, 1894, oil on canvas, 39⅜ x 25⅝ in. (100 x 65 cm), Museum of Fine Arts, Boston

Rouen Cathedral, 1894, oil on canvas, 39⅜ x 28¾ in. (100 x 73 cm), Musée d'Orsay, Paris

Happy Times in Giverny:

The family at Giverny, photograph, collection Toulgouat-Piguet, Vernon

Jean-Pierre and Michel, the youngest, photograph, collection Toulgouat-Piguet, Vernon

Ice-skating on the Epte, photograph, collection Toulgouat-Piguet, Vernon

The house at Giverny, photograph

Boat on the Epte, 1890, oil on canvas, 52⅜ x 57⅛ in. (133 x 145 cm), Museo de Arte de São Paulo; Photographie Giraudon, Vanves

Travels:

Claude and Alice in the Piazza San Marco in Venice, photograph 1908

The Houses of Parliament, London, Sun through Fog, 1904, oil on canvas, 31⅞ x 36¼ in. (81 x 92 cm), Musée d'Orsay, Paris

Charing Cross Bridge, the Thames (detail), 1903, oil on canvas, 28¾ x 39⅜ in. (73 x 100 cm), Musée des Beaux-Arts, Lyon

Monet in the car he bought in 1900 and which he drove over the Alps to Saint Moritz — in winter, photograph *c.* 1900, collection Toulgouat-Piguet, Vernon

Palazzo Contarini del Zaffo, Venice, 1908, oil on canvas, 36¼ x 31⅞ in. (92 x 81 cm), Kunstmuseum St. Gallen

The Water Lilies:

The lily pond at Giverny, postcard

Monet, painting the lily pond, with Blanche, photograph 8 July 1915, collection Piguet, Paris

Water Lilies (detail), 1916–19, oil on canvas, 59 x 77½ in. (150 x 197 cm), The Art Institute of Chicago

The Japanese Bridge:

The Lily Pond, the Japanese Bridge (detail), 1899, oil on canvas, 35 x 36¼ in. (89 x 92 cm), The Trustees of the National Gallery, London

Hokusai
People on a Bridge (detail), *c.* 1835/36, wood cut, 35 x 39⅜ in. (89 x 100 cm), The Art Institute of Chicago

Monet near the Japanese Bridge, photograph

The Japanese Bridge, 1918–24, oil on canvas, 35 x 29⅞ in. (89 x 100 cm), Musée Marmottan, Paris

Farewell:

Monet after an eye operation in February 1923, photograph

View of Giverny, photograph 1926

Monet's funeral procession, photograph, 8 December 1926

Right:

Path in Monet's Garden (detail), 1901–02, oil on canvas, 35 x 36¼ in. (89 x 92 cm), Österreichische Galerie, Vienna; Photography: Fotostudio Otto, Vienna

Back Cover:

Monet seated on a bench, photograph, International Museum of Photography, George Eastman House, New York

© 2023, Prestel Verlag, Munich · London · New York
A member of Penguin Random House Verlagsgruppe GmbH
Neumarkter Strasse 28 · 81673 Munich

Library of Congress Control Number: 2023933360
A CIP catalogue record for this book is available from the British Library.

Text by Stephan Koja and Katja Miksovsky

Translated from German by Andrea P. A. Belloli

Design and layout: Susanne Rüber
Production management: Susanne Hermann
Lithography: Karl Dörfel, Munich
Printing and binding: Printer Trento, Trento

Our production is climate neutral
ClimatePartner.com/14044-1912-1001
Print product

Prestel Publishing compensates the CO_2 emissions produced from the making of this book by supporting a reforestation project in Brazil. Find further information on the project here:
www.ClimatePartner.com/14044-1912-1001

Penguin Random House Verlagsgruppe FSC® N001967

Printed in Italy

ISBN 978-3-7913-7568-7

www.prestel.com